## DATE DUE

|  |  |  |  |
|---|---|---|---|
|  |  |  |  |
|  |  |  |  |
|  |  |  |  |
|  |  |  |  |
|  |  |  |  |
|  |  |  |  |
|  |  |  |  |
|  |  |  |  |

# WHY SHOULD I BRUSH MY TEETH?

✦ and other questions about healthy teeth ✦

## Louise Spilsbury

Heinemann Library
Chicago, Illinois

Customer Service  888-454-2279

Visit our website at www.heinemannlibrary.com

Designed by David Poole and Tokay Interactive Ltd
Illustrations by Kamae Design Ltd
Originated by Ambassador Litho Ltd
Printed in China by W K T

07 06
10 9 8 7 6 5 4 3 2

**Library of Congress Cataloging-in-Publication Data**
Spilsbury, Louise.
  Why should I brush my teeth? : and other questions about healthy teeth
  / Louise Spilsbury.
      v. cm. --  (Body matters)
Includes bibliographical references and index.
Contents: Why are healthy teeth important? -- What are teeth made of? --
Why are there different kinds of teeth -- Why are sweets bad for my
teeth? -- Why does my tooth hurt? -- Why Should I brush my teeth? -- How
do dentists help? -- Why do I have to wear braces? -- Why does my breath
smell bad? -- Amazing facts about teeth.
  ISBN 1-4034-4679-2 (HC)
  1.  Teeth--Care and hygiene--Juvenile literature. 2.  Teeth--Juvenile
literature. [1. Teeth. 2. Teeth--Care and hygiene.] I. Title. II.
Series.
  RK63.S665 2003
  617.6'01--dc21
                           2003004984

**Acknowledgments**
The author and publishers are grateful to the following for permission to reproduce copyright material:
p. 4 Corbis/Reflections Photo Library: Jennie Woodcock; pp. 5, 8, 11, 12, 15, 16, 17, 23, 24, 26 Science Photo Library; pp. 6, 14, 18, 27, 28 Tudor Photography; pp. 9, 10, 25 Getty Images/Stone; p. 13 Trevor Clifford; p. 19 Getty Images; p. 20 Corbis/Jon Feingersh; p. 21 Corbis/Rob Lewine; p. 22 Photodisc.

Cover photograph by Tudor Photography.

Every effort has been made to contact copyright holders of any material reproduced in this book. Any omissions will be rectified in subsequent printings if notice is given to the publisher.

Some words are shown in bold, **like this.** You can find out what they mean by looking in the glossary.

# CONTENTS

# WHY ARE HEALTHY TEETH IMPORTANT?

"Smile and the world smiles with you"—or so the saying goes. Sadly, people are less likely to smile back at you if you present them with a mouth full of neglected teeth. So, having a nice smile is one reason you should look after your teeth. But what else do teeth do for us?

## Eat up

Teeth are responsible for the first stage in the process of digestion—the way your body breaks down the food you eat into pieces small enough for it to use to make **energy.** Your teeth bite off chunks of food and chew and crush them into smaller pieces that your body can digest. Without teeth, it would be difficult to eat anything other than soft foods, such as soup and mashed potatoes.

Healthy teeth are strong and tough and can bite through crunchy and hard foods, such as apples and nuts.

## Talking teeth

You may not realize it, but when you talk, you use your teeth. Teeth are an important part of the way you communicate because they help you to speak clearly. In fact, you cannot make the sounds of some of the letters of the alphabet, such as f, t, and v, without the help of your teeth. Try saying "I've got terrific teeth" without them!

## Reasons to brush

If you do not take care of your teeth, they soon begin to look dirty. And they not only look bad—they feel bad, too. Toothache is the word used to describe the pain we feel when we have problems with teeth. A toothache can be very painful. It can make it hard for you to concentrate on anything.

Your teeth are very important. Athletes who play sports in which they may get hit in the mouth wear a mouth guard like this to protect their teeth.

# WHAT ARE TEETH MADE OF?

Your teeth have to be very tough to stand up to all the chewing, biting, and gnawing you put them through every day. They are covered in a shiny, white layer called **enamel.** This is the hardest substance in your body—harder even than bone. But the enamel is only a small part of what makes a tooth.

## Crowns and roots

A tooth is made up of two main sections—one that you can see and another that you cannot.

When you look in your mouth, you can see your pink gums and the white crowns of your teeth.

When you open your mouth, you can see the **crown.** This is the part outside of the **gums.** The other part of the tooth—the **root**—is hidden inside the gums. The root is up to two-thirds of the tooth's total length. It holds the tooth firmly in the jawbone.

# The different parts of a tooth

The white enamel on the outside of a tooth is a hard covering that protects the softer parts inside the tooth from the wear and tear of chewing and biting.

**Dentine** is a yellow layer beneath the enamel. It is slightly softer than enamel but is as hard as bone. It acts like a hard cushion, absorbing some of the shock that might get to the inner tooth when you bite something hard or hit your mouth on something.

Blood vessels bring your teeth nourishment that your body has made from your food.

The **pulp** is a spongy layer at the center of the tooth. It contains blood vessels and **nerves**.

The gum is the pink material around the tooth. Part of the tooth is above the gum and part is below.

bone

Nerves carry signals to your brain—for example, to tell you when a tooth is hurt.

The tooth root is held in place in the jawbone by tough fibers and a substance called cementum, a kind of natural cement.

# WHY ARE THERE DIFFERENT KINDS OF TEETH?

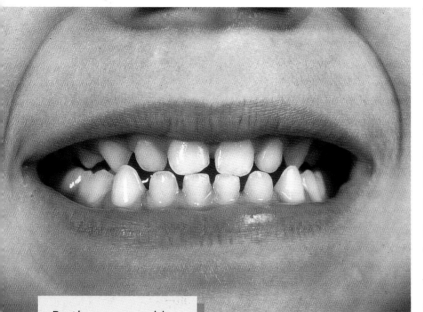

By three years old, a child should have all of his or her twenty baby teeth.

When a baby is born, it looks as if he or she has no teeth. In fact, tiny teeth are already there, hidden in the **gums** and already partly grown. The first teeth to emerge (come out) are called baby teeth. These start to emerge when babies are about six or seven months old. After about five years, baby teeth begin to fall out and permanent teeth start to grow.

## What are baby teeth?

Your first teeth are called baby teeth because they emerge while you are still a baby. You do not need big, tough teeth when you are very young because you do not eat hard, solid food then. For this reason, baby teeth are smaller and weaker than adult teeth. These smaller teeth also fit better in a baby's small mouth.

## Why do we have baby teeth?

Baby teeth are very important. They help you chew food and form sounds when you learn to talk. Baby teeth also guide the permanent teeth that grow after them into the right place in your mouth. If baby teeth fall out too early, adult teeth may grow too closely together, which makes them hard to clean properly.

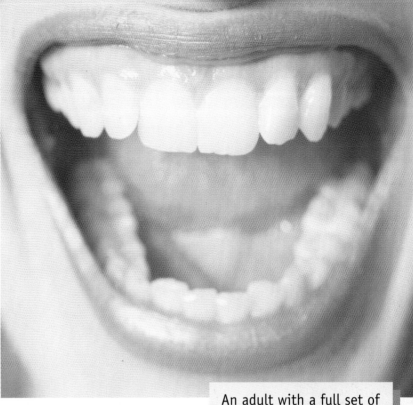

An adult with a full set of permanent teeth has 32 in all— 16 on the top and 16 on the bottom.

## Permanent teeth

The word *permanent* means lasting forever, and your permanent teeth have to last for the rest of your life. If you lose a permanent tooth, through an accident or because of **decay,** you will be left with a gap because there are no new teeth buds left in the gums to grow in its place.

9

## Why are teeth different shapes?

Our teeth are different shapes because they have different jobs to do. It is like the different tools cooks use—they have one kind of knife for carving meat and another to slice bread. Humans are omnivores—we eat meat, fruit, and vegetables. Adults have three different kinds of teeth for cutting, tearing, and chewing these different kinds of food.

The fanglike teeth near the front of the mouth are called canines. They are good for tearing food.

## Incisors and canines

The four front teeth at the top and bottom of your mouth have straight, sharp ends. They are called **incisors,** and we use them to bite into and slice through food. On each side of the incisors is a tooth with a long, sharp point. These are the **canine** teeth. They are used for tearing off bits of food.

## Molars for chewing

The teeth at the back of your mouth behind the canines, have wide, flat tops that feel bumpy to your tongue. These are the **molars.** Molars are used to crush and chew food. They grind up food into pieces small enough for you to swallow comfortably.

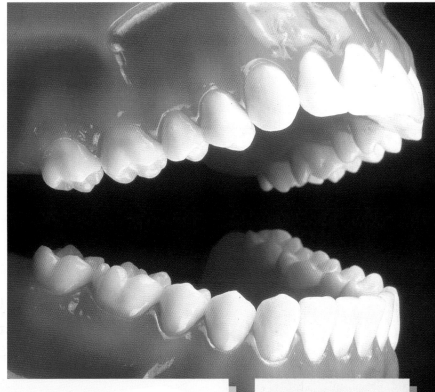

### WHAT ARE WISDOM TEETH?

In spite of their name, these are not teeth that only grow if you study hard! They got their name because they are the last teeth to appear —they usually grow when you are about twenty years old. Most people have four wisdom teeth, one in each corner of the mouth. Your wisdom teeth are also known as your third molars because they are a type of molar.

Your teeth have particular shapes because they have different jobs to do when you eat. Think about how they work next time you have a meal.

11

# WHY ARE SWEETS BAD FOR MY TEETH?

Sweets are bad for your teeth because they contain lots of sugar, which is what makes them taste sweet. When sugar sticks to a sticky layer on your teeth called **plaque,** it can damage your teeth. This is called tooth **decay.**

## What is plaque?

Plaque is the main cause of tooth decay and **gum disease.** Plaque is a thin layer of **bacteria.** It forms on all teeth, especially near the **gums,** between teeth, and on the back of the teeth.

Special chewable pills turn plaque blue to show you how much plaque is on your teeth and where it collects the most.

Bacteria in plaque change the sugars in food and drink into **acid.** Acid is a very strong substance that can wear away a tooth's **enamel,** and enamel cannot repair itself or grow back.

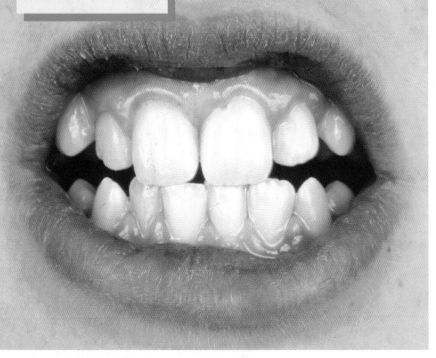

# What is gum disease?

The bacteria in plaque can harm your gums as well as your teeth. Gum disease is an **infection** caused by the bacteria. It makes gums red, sore, and swollen, and they may bleed a little when you brush your teeth. Gum disease can also weaken your gums, making it harder for them to hold your teeth in place.

Sweets that stay in your mouth a long time, such as lollipops, are the worst kinds because they allow plaque to make more acid.

## WHAT DOES SALIVA DO?

Saliva is another word for the spit in your mouth. Saliva helps protect your teeth. It washes away food and bacteria that collect on your teeth and gums. Saliva can also limit the damage that acid does to teeth. If you leave a two- or three-hour gap between meals, saliva can mix with some of the acid and make it harmless.

Watch out for juices and other drinks. Some claim to be healthy, when they really contain lots of sugar. Check the list of ingredients on the back, and try drinking water or milk instead!

## HEALTHY SNACKS

Here are some ideas for snacks that taste good and do not contain sugar: plain yogurt, nuts and seeds, raw vegetables (such as carrot sticks), bread, pretzels, whole-wheat cereals (check that they do not have added sugar), and cheese.

## Are other foods bad for my teeth?

Sugars are in all sorts of foods, not just sweets. Any foods that contain lots of sugar, such as cakes and soda, can cause tooth **decay** if you eat too much of them. Hard and chewy sweets are especially bad, because they can also stain your teeth. Try to save sweet foods for occasional treats.

# What foods are good for my teeth?

To keep your teeth—and the rest of your body—healthy, you need to eat a variety of different foods. You should eat some carbohydrates—such as potatoes, pasta, or rice—at every meal, and try to have at least five different fruits and vegetables each day. You also need small amounts of **protein-**rich foods, such as nuts, meat, milk, and cheese.

Milk and foods made from milk, such as cheese and yogurt, are especially good for your teeth because they contain calcium. Calcium is one of the substances that make up the hard parts of your teeth. Your body can use calcium from food and drinks to help build strong teeth and keep them that way.

Milk contains calcium to help keep your teeth strong. It has other vitamins and minerals that help keep the rest of your body healthy.

# WHY DOES MY TOOTH HURT?

Your tooth hurts when the **acid** made by the **bacteria** in **plaque** burns a hole through the protective layer of **enamel** on the tooth's surface. As the hole gets bigger, it reaches the more sensitive layers of the tooth. When these are exposed to the air, you get a toothache.

## How does it happen?

A hole in your tooth is called a **cavity.** After a cavity forms, food and bacteria get lodged in the hole when you eat. The bacteria gather there under the enamel, and make more and more acid. This acid wears away the part of the tooth below the enamel— the **dentine.** Soon the hole may go all the way to the **pulp** at the center of the tooth.

This photo of a tooth cavity has been magnified so you can see it. Cavities can cause a lot of pain.

## When does it hurt?

The enamel layer does not have any **nerves** in it, so it cannot feel pain. The dentine has some nerves in it, and the pulp has many. When something cold, such as an iced drink, passes over the hole, the cold reaches these nerves and you feel pain.

If you get a toothache, you should see a dentist as soon as possible. The dentist will be able to help you and stop the pain.

## WHY DO NERVES FEEL PAIN?

Nerves carry messages between the different parts of your body and your brain. Pain is one of the messages they carry. A toothache may not feel very nice, but it does a useful job. It tells your brain (and, therefore, you) that you have a cavity. You know that you need to see a dentist, who can fix it before it gets any worse!

17

# WHY SHOULD I BRUSH MY TEETH?

Brushing your teeth cleans off the layer of **plaque** that builds up on them. It also removes the bits of food that the **bacteria** in plaque feed on to make **acid.** Plaque is actually quite soft and easy to get rid of if you clean your teeth properly and often.

Some people check their watch or use a timer to make sure that they brush their teeth for two minutes. You could try brushing your teeth for the length of your favorite song.

## How often should I brush my teeth?

If possible, brush your teeth after each time that you eat, especially if you snack on something sweet and sticky, such as dried fruit. If you cannot do that, brush your teeth at least twice a day—after breakfast and before you go to bed. Do not rush your brushing—keep cleaning for at least two minutes.

## What is the best way to brush teeth?

First, squeeze a small amount of toothpaste no bigger than a small pea onto your toothbrush. Then, get your toothbrush wet. Put the brush onto the tooth at an angle and brush up and down, making tiny circles with the brush as you move it. Make sure that you clean outside the whole tooth—back, front, and sides. Clean one or two teeth at a time and make sure that you move the toothbrush to clean each one properly. Jiggle the brush over the **gums** and the roof of the mouth to get them clean.

Wash your toothbrush in clean, cold water after using it. Then shake it and stand it upright so that it can dry in the air.

Be careful not to brush too hard. This can damage tooth **enamel** and push your gums higher, which might expose part of the **root.**

19

## What kind of toothbrush should I use?

It is important to use a toothbrush that is right for you. Choose a brush that has soft bristles with rounded ends because these will not hurt your **gums.** A small brush head is best because it can reach all the parts of your mouth easily. A long, wide handle helps you get a good grip. Many dentists recommend using an electric toothbrush.

## What is dental floss?

Dental floss is thin, waxy string that helps you remove **plaque** and bits of food your toothbrush cannot reach. Holding a long piece, slip the floss between your teeth with a seesaw movement, being careful not to push it hard against the gums. Then, slide it down and out, bringing bits of plaque and food with it.

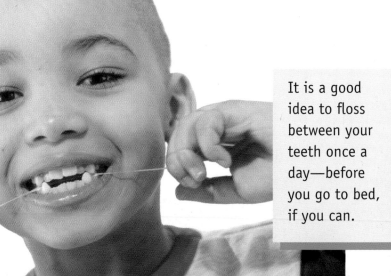

It is a good idea to floss between your teeth once a day—before you go to bed, if you can.

## How often should I change my toothbrush?

You should change your toothbrush (or toothbrush head, if you use an electric toothbrush) when the bristles begin to spread. For most people, this means every two or three months. Bristles that are out of shape will not clean your teeth properly. Also, **bacteria** can build up in old toothbrushes and cause **infections,** such as **gum disease.**

If you become ill, get a new toothbrush and change it again when you are better. The **germs** that made you ill collect on your toothbrush and could make you sick again.

## WHAT IS IN TOOTHPASTE?

Toothpastes have several ingredients, including flavorings, stuff to make them foam up, and cleaners that rub away plaque. Most contain fluoride, a mineral that helps prevent tooth **decay** and strengthen **enamel.** Too much fluoride is not good for you, though, so always spit out your toothpaste after brushing.

# HOW DO DENTISTS HELP?

A dentist is a kind of doctor who has had a lot of training and experience in taking care of people's teeth. As well as checking your teeth and **gums** to find out if they have any problems, dentists also make sure that your teeth are growing properly. Everyone should visit a dentist every six months for a checkup to make sure that their teeth stay healthy.

Your dentist asks you to open your mouth wide so he or she can examine your teeth carefully.

## What happens at a checkup?

In the dentist's office, you will sit in a large, padded chair. This chair can move you up and lean you back so that the dentist can get a good view of your teeth. The dentist shines a bright light into your mouth and may use a tiny mirror to look all around your teeth and gums.

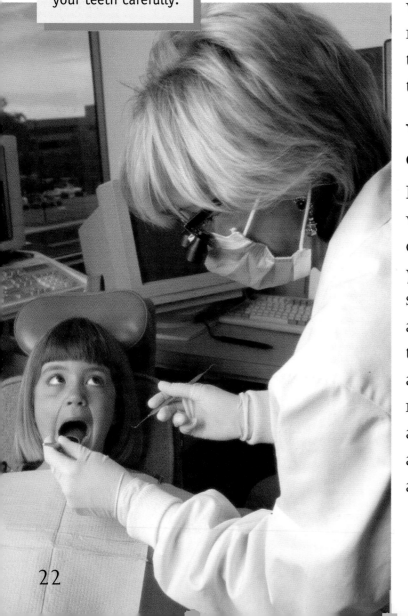

The dentist also checks that your top and bottom teeth work together when you close your mouth to bite. If they do not, or if your teeth are too close together, too far apart, or crooked, you may need to see an **orthodontist.** An orthodontist is a kind of dentist who can correct the shape or position of your teeth.

## What do X rays of my teeth show?

After checking your mouth carefully, the dentist may take an X ray of your teeth. X rays are pictures that can show if there are any **cavities** in your teeth that the dentist could not see. They can also show problems with your gums.

The X-ray machine takes a picture of a part of your mouth while you bite down on a piece of plastic. The plastic holds the X-ray film on which the picture will show.

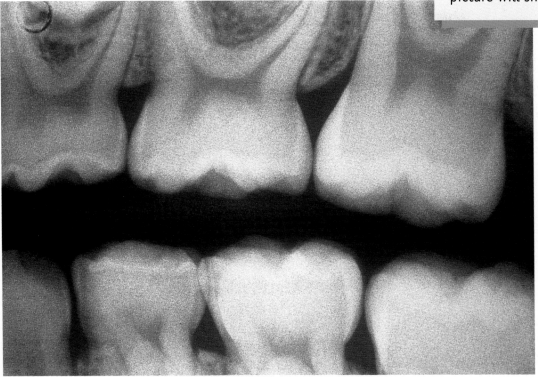

## What if I have a cavity?

If you have a **cavity,** your dentist can fix it. The dentist takes out the rotten part of the tooth with a tiny drill and other special tools. Then he or she fills the hole with a type of white cement or a kind of silver metal. The filling is shaped so it feels just like your real teeth.

Before starting, the dentist gives the area around the tooth an anesthetic. This is a medicine that makes the area go numb so that you cannot feel anything there.

Before you get a filling, the dentist will usually give you an injection so you cannot feel the drill.

After the filling is done, your mouth may continue feeling numb and a little strange for a few hours. The dentist will tell you not to eat anything until your mouth is back to normal and the filling has gotten completely hard.

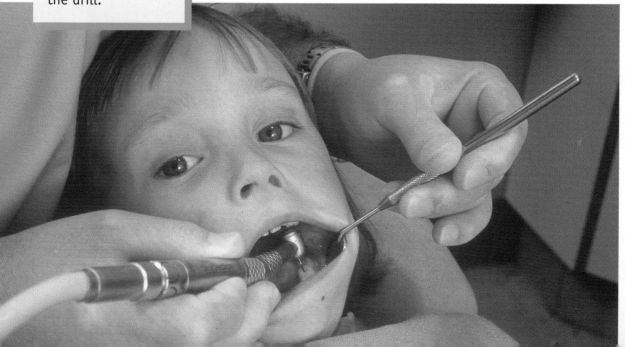

## What does a dental hygienist do?

Dental hygienists are experts at keeping teeth and **gums** clean and healthy. Their job is to clean and polish teeth. They use a scraper to remove any **plaque** that you have not been able to get rid of. Then they brush and polish your teeth with a special brush and paste to make them really clean.

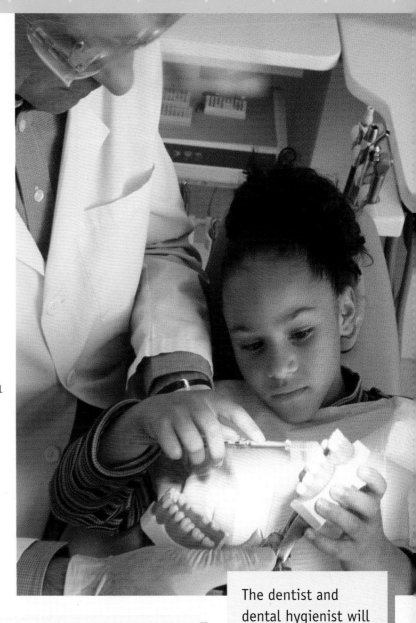

The dentist and dental hygienist will teach you the right way to brush and floss your teeth.

## WHAT IS TOOTH SEALANT?

Dentists sometimes protect teeth with a special sealant. Some teeth, especially the **molars,** are hard to clean, and food and **bacteria** collect in them. Sealant is a very thin layer of a kind of plastic that protects a tooth from **decay.**

# WHY DO I HAVE TO WEAR BRACES?

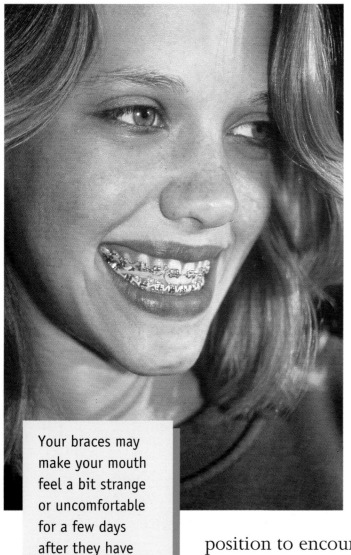

Your braces may make your mouth feel a bit strange or uncomfortable for a few days after they have been fitted, but most people soon get used to them.

Many people—both children and adults—wear braces. **Orthodontists** fit braces to make a person's teeth grow straight if they are too close together, too far apart, crooked, or if they do not meet properly when the mouth is closed.

## How do braces work?

First, a small bracket, usually made from metal, is fixed to each tooth. Next, a wire or band is attached to the brackets. The dentist then bends the length of wire into the shape that the teeth should be. The wire holds the teeth firmly in this position to encourage them to grow straight. Most people have to go back every few weeks so that the orthodontist can adjust the wire as the teeth slowly change position.

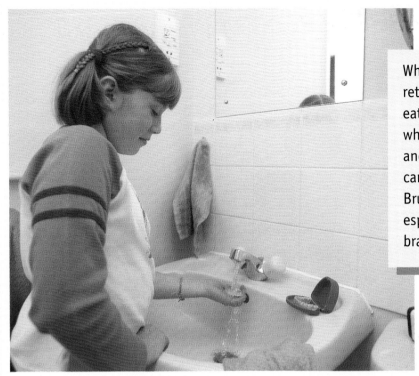

## What are retainers?

After you have worn braces for long enough, the orthodontist may suggest that you wear a retainer for a while. This is a small piece of hard plastic with metal wires—it is like braces that you can put in and take out. It is shaped to fit your newly straightened teeth, and it makes sure they stay in their correct position. Some people only need to wear retainers to straighten their teeth.

## KINDS OF BRACES

You can choose from many different kinds of braces. There are clear braces made from plastic and braces that fit behind the teeth so they cannot be seen. You can get braces with different colored bands or wires—some people change colors for different occasions!

# WHY DOES MY BREATH SMELL BAD?

Bad breath can happen for lots of different reasons—for example, when you have a cold or when you eat certain foods, such as garlic and onions. Most people get bad breath if they have not been taking care of their teeth.

Bacteria can grow on your tongue, and cause a bad smell. When you brush your teeth, gently scrub your tongue, too.

## How can I prevent bad breath?

If **plaque** and **bacteria** build up in your mouth, they can begin to rot a tooth, and this makes it smell. Bits of food stuck between your teeth become smelly if you do not remove them. Solve these problems by brushing your teeth properly and regularly, using dental floss to get rid of trapped food and plaque, and visiting the dentist twice a year. That way, your smile should stay sparkling and your breath fresh!

# AMAZING FACTS ABOUT TEETH

- Your teeth started forming before you were even born, and they were in your **gums** when you were born.

- All mammals have two types of teeth during their lives—baby teeth and, later, permanent teeth.

- The teeth are the only part of the human body that cannot repair themselves.

- The hardest substance in your whole body is the **enamel** on your teeth.

- Many people think of football and hockey as the most dangerous sports for mouths and teeth. In fact, four out of ten mouth injuries happen when people are playing basketball and baseball!

- The most common disease in the world today is tooth **decay.**

- The first toothbrush to look anything like the ones you use today was invented in China 1,000 years ago. The bristles were made from the hairs of a horse's mane and the handle was made from ivory (elephant tusk).

# GLOSSARY

**acid** substance strong enough to burn through tooth enamel

**bacteria** tiny living things that can cause disease

**canines** long, sharp, pointed teeth that grow on either side of the incisors

**cavity** hole where a tooth has decayed

**crown** part of the tooth outside of the gums

**decay** when the enamel of a tooth is worn away

**dentine** yellow, bonelike layer of the tooth found beneath the enamel

**enamel** hard, white outer covering of a tooth

**energy** power that living things need for everything they do

**germs** bacteria and other tiny living things that can cause disease

**gum disease** infection caused by the bacteria in plaque. It makes gums red, sore, and swollen.

**gums** pink part of the mouth around the teeth

**incisors** front teeth used for slicing and cutting food

**infection** kind of disease that can be spread to other people

**molars** flat-topped teeth at the back of the mouth used to chew food

**nerves** passageways that carry messages to and from the brain

**orthodontist** special kind of dentist who corrects the shape or position of the teeth

**plaque** thin, sticky layer that grows on the teeth

**protein** substance in some foods that the body can use to build or repair body parts

**pulp** spongy layer at the center of the tooth that contains blood vessels and nerves

**root** part of the tooth that holds it firmly in the jawbone

# FURTHER READING

McGinty, Alice. *Good Hygiene*. Danbury, Conn.: Franklin Watts, 1999.

Royston, Angela. *Healthy Teeth*. Chicago: Heinemann Library, 2003.

Stewart, Alex. *Keeping Clean*. Danbury, Conn.: Scholastic Library, 2000.

# INDEX